IMAGINEERING

7 Success Principles To Engineer
Your Imagination

VINISHA JAYASWAL

Chennai • Bangalore

CLEVER FOX PUBLISHING
Chennai, India

Published by CLEVER FOX PUBLISHING 2024
Copyright © VINISHA JAYASWAL 2024

All Rights Reserved.
ISBN: 978-93-56486-96-6

This book has been published with all reasonable efforts taken to make the material error-free after the consent of the author. No part of this book shall be used, reproduced in any manner whatsoever without written permission from the author, except in the case of brief quotations embodied in critical articles and reviews.

The Author of this book is solely responsible and liable for its content including but not limited to the views, representations, descriptions, statements, information, opinions and references ["Content"]. The Content of this book shall not constitute or be construed or deemed to reflect the opinion or expression of the Publisher or Editor. Neither the Publisher nor Editor endorse or approve the Content of this book or guarantee the reliability, accuracy or completeness of the Content published herein and do not make any representations or warranties of any kind, express or implied, including but not limited to the implied warranties of merchantability, fitness for a particular purpose. The Publisher and Editor shall not be liable whatsoever for any errors, omissions, whether such errors or omissions result from negligence, accident, or any other cause or claims for loss or damages of any kind, including without limitation, indirect or consequential loss or damage arising out of use, inability to use, or about the reliability, accuracy or sufficiency of the information contained in this book.

Dedication

To my dear parents, who have always been my guiding light and source of inspiration.

Thank you for instilling in me the values of hard work, perseverance, and determination and for believing in me even when I didn't believe in myself.

To my loving husband, who has been my rock and constant companion. Your unwavering support and encouragement have helped me overcome every obstacle and reach for the stars.

And finally, to my dearest son, who brings joy and meaning to my life every day. I hope this book will inspire you to pursue your dreams and passions, just as you have inspired me to be the best version of myself.

Thank you, from the bottom of my heart, for being my pillars of strength and always standing by my side.

DON'T QUIT

"When things go wrong, as they sometimes will,
When the road you're trudging seems all uphill,
When the funds are low and the debts are high,
And you want to smile, but you have to sigh,
When care is pressing you down a bit,
Rest, if you must, but don't you quit.

Life is queer with its twists and turns,
As every one of us sometimes learns,
And many a failure turns about,
When he might have won had he stuck it out;
Don't give up though the pace seems slow-
You may succeed with another blow.

Often the goal is nearer than,
It seems to a faint and faltering man,
Often the struggler has given up,
When he might have captured the Victor's cup,
And he learned too late when the night slipped down,
How close he was to the golden crown.

Success is failure turned inside out-
The silver tint of the clouds of doubt,
And you never can tell how close you are,
It may be near when it seems so far,
So stick to the fight when you're hardest hit-
It's when things seem worst that you must not quit."

– Edgar A. Guest

MEET THE AUTHOR

Hello, my name is Vinisha Jayaswal. I am a transformational coach, neuro-linguistic practitioner, Pranic healer, process facilitator, corporate trainer, organizational development professional and now an author.

My 20+ year career highlights my experience across various domains.

I have evolved into a seasoned learning and organization development professional with personalised and dynamic leadership skills.

My expertise has fruition from delivering multiple and sustained organisational growths in diverse environments, establishing structure, building employee value, and driving vision. All of this is aimed at achieving critical pre-set strategic goals.

That focus has resulted in my becoming an organizational development and transformational specialist. My work has been appreciated for my ability to design and facilitate change interventions and coach leaders. I believe and excel in seamlessly aligning stakeholders and attaining results by focusing on customer centricity. This has helped organisations and individuals thrive with the best learning strategies.

Having said that, I am a hands-on leader, which has helped me manage and drive a digital process and cultural transformation to make future-ready hospitals across healthcare.

I am considered to be a motivational speaker and trainer of high repute. My facilitation skills/training programs and executive coaching sessions are widely appreciated because of their high-quality content coupled with a unique thought-provoking, stimulating and entertaining delivery style. I ensure all this with an enduring commitment towards excellence.

An enthusiastic professional with a proven ability in coaching leaders, learning and development and imparting various training and facilitation programs, I combine active learning, objectivity and fun to the program.

My core competencies lie in coaching, customer centricity, behavioural and soft skill Training, Process facilitation and a renewed passion for achieving success. I pride myself on being a very determined, focused and delivery-oriented professional who brings tremendous value addition to the table.

My philosophy is that - To transform others, one must constantly be on the self-transformation journey.

Hence, I constantly up my skills, learn, un-learn, and transform. This constant self-upskilling process has led me to win many national and international awards.

This book, 'Imagineering', is a coaching program which I created to help individuals in organizations achieve success in all endeavors of their life.

My mission is to help 10 million people find and do everything that makes them successful. Giving people a sense of purpose or feeling valued brings out the best in them.

FOREWORD

*I*nnovation and creativity have become the cornerstones of progress, and the ability to harness the power of imagination is more critical than ever. Disruption has been at a scale that has been unimagined. The world is fast changing, and all we need is some anchors for us to understand what it means to dream, to imagine and to bring to life what we conceive of. I was pleasantly surprised to see the author, Vinisha Jayaswal, put together a super exciting book, *Imagineering - 7 Success Principles to Engineer Your Imagination*. It is a masterful guide that offers a profound and transformative journey into the realm of imaginative thinking. This book isn't just a manual for unlocking your creative potential; it's a blueprint for crafting a life filled with success, fulfilment, and boundless possibilities.

The author, a coach in the field of imagination engineering, takes you on a captivating voyage through the corridors of the mind, revealing the secret to turning the intangible into the tangible. It's not just a book; it's a roadmap to reinvigorating your creativity, sparking innovation, and turning your wildest dreams into reality. In a world inundated with the noise of the mundane, *Imagineering* stands out as a lighthouse, guiding you towards your true potential. The principles within these pages are not just theories but the author's own time-tested, actionable insights that can help you engineer your imagination for remarkable success in all areas of life. From business ventures to personal relationships, from artistic endeavours to scientific breakthroughs, this book has the power to transform how you approach challenges and opportunities.

The seven principles outlined here are not mere guidelines; they are powerful tools that can help you harness the creative energy that resides within you. As you delve into each principle, you'll discover a wealth of knowledge and practical techniques to ignite your inner vision. This book is not about simply dreaming–it's about taking action to manifest those dreams into a tangible reality.

Imagineering is a holistic guide that underscores the importance of balance between logical reasoning and imaginative thinking. It celebrates the synergy of both worlds, encouraging you to bridge the gap between the left and right brain and cultivate a harmonious relationship between your analytical and creative faculties. It's not just about imagining; it's about engineering those dreams into existence, making the seemingly impossible possible.

I invite you to embark on this exhilarating journey through the corridors of creativity and imagination. With *Imagineering - 7 Success Principles to Engineer Your Imagination* as your guide, you'll learn to paint your own canvas of success, one vibrant stroke at a time. Whether you are an entrepreneur seeking innovation, an artist searching for inspiration, or an individual striving for personal growth, this book offers the tools to engineer your imagination and sculpt your destiny.

As you delve into the pages of *Imagineering*, prepare to be inspired, motivated, and, above all, empowered to unleash the limitless potential of your imagination. The world is waiting for your unique creations, and this book is the key to unlocking your imagination's boundless horizons.

With great enthusiasm, I encourage you to embrace the profound wisdom within these pages and embark on a transformative journey towards becoming the ultimate Imagineer of your life. I certainly plan to get on the wings of imagination and with these tools, I believe success will become a vivid reality!

SV Nathan
Partner, Deloitte India

PREFACE

*I*t all began in 2004 when I had just started my journey of becoming a trainer in the corporate world. I joined an ITES company along with four other trainers. We were all freshers in the training industry and were being trained to become trainers. Three weeks later, I fell ill and could not get to work for the next four weeks.

By the time I returned to work, all my other colleagues who joined along with me were already at client sites, conducting training. I was the only fresher left in the office. I waited for a senior trainer to train me and bring me up to speed with the rest of my colleagues. At that time, I did not know that something like this never took place in the corporate world. If you miss the bus, you have to catch up on your own.

So, I started learning in my own way. A week later, on a Thursday evening, as I was packing up to go home, Diana, the managing director, called and asked me if I would do a one-day training session on communication skills at a client site. The training was on the following Saturday, which was the day after.

I realized that this was my only opportunity to go out and start training. If I did not agree to go and conduct the training, I would end up sitting in the office waiting forever.

So, I agreed, and she told me that Neena, a senior trainer, would prepare me for it the next day. Hence, at work, Neena and I sat making the PowerPoint presentations the next day, which almost took us the whole day. I was just following what she said. She ran me through the entire eight-hour training program in a couple of hours, and I had to deliver that the next day.

The day had arrived–my first-ever training program. It was the first time I had ever faced such a large audience. My palms were sweaty, and my heart thumped as I walked to the training room. The participants were already seated in the room. I had 30 pairs of eyes looking at me. I felt very conscious. I tried to calm myself and show that I was not nervous.

So, I started on time and within two hours, I had completed the eight-hour training program. Errrrggg….I finished everything I remembered of what Neena took me through.

Neena panicked and called Diana and informed her of what had happened. I was scared and thought that was my last day at work.

Well, Neena took over and completed the training program.

When I reached the office, Diana confronted me. She understood that the team should have prepared me more before I went out. As a result, I was not sent out for the next four months, preparing on my own, shadowing other trainers and seeking help as and when trainers came back from a client site.

Four months later, I was sent for a ten-day program to a client site and was evaluated for the same by a senior trainer. I made a few mistakes, but overall, I did well.

So what then changed here for me? What did I do that made me do well?

I started to believe that ***it was up to me to make a difference in my career. And I am solely responsible for it.***

So, I started setting goals and also achieving them. One year down the line, I received a 40% increment in my salary, the highest increment that the company had ever given anyone.

Goal after goal I set and achieved, and in two years, I was responsible for training the trainers who joined the company. I became a senior trainer and an asset to the organization. I created the best version of myself. After that, there was no looking back. I kept developing the best versions of myself each time, competing with myself and no others.

As the years went by and I kept achieving all the goals I set for myself, I also began to learn and relearn. I didn't just want to sit in one place and let life make choices for me, but I wanted to make my own choices in life.

I decided to live a life by choice, not by chance.

Imagineering is about engineering your mind to live your life by choice and succeed in everything you do.

I have experienced many challenges in health at different stages in my life. As a transformational coach, corporate trainer, pranic healer and neuro-linguistic practitioner (NLP), I have seen others suffer too.

Our bodies express what's happening inside our minds and emotions. Any disturbance in our lives can lead to DIS-EASE. Wellness is holistic. It is a 360-degree transition. It should give us success in every area of life with joy and freedom of living.

During my research, I came to several conclusions that led me to conclude that the emotions we want to feel are the root of every issue in our lives. Since then, I've been coaching to motivate people to discover the true purpose of their lives. I saw them feeling fulfilled at every turn as they started this journey, which made me feel even more fulfilled because I felt like I was contributing to something bigger than myself.

To live a life of fulfilment is our birth right and not a luxury offered to a lucky few. Everyone is entitled to feel fulfilled by the work we do, the life we lead, our relationships, and the lifestyle and legacy we are creating. We have to wake up every single day feeling inspired to live every moment with joy and freedom and feel significant every moment that we have contributed to something larger than ourselves. Our days and moments should be filled with love and happiness so that we feel limitless to love what we do and do what we love.

My journey and this book are about inspiring people to succeed in all walks of life.

My life mission is to help people find and do all those things that make them successful in their life. Giving people a sense of purpose or feeling valued brings out the best in them.

During my training, I learnt the concept of microcosm and macrocosm.

The whole universe comprises five elements, and so are all living beings. A pattern, nature, and structure similarity exists between humans and the universe. This concept of microcosm and macrocosm views humans as a more miniature representation of the universe. The five elements of life are earth, water, fire, air, and space. At the same time, every life has its recipe and combination. We all have similar challenges, but to overcome them, one needs to identify the key to open this lock or their unique code to find solutions. For centuries and in every ancient philosophy, the soul and the body were conceived as one fused existence.

If all this is true, we and the universe are in constant harmony, whether it's pain or pleasure.

"What we are is what we represent in our universe."

So, to experience a better world, we must become a better version of ourselves. To live this complete life of freedom and joy, how can you bring more of yourself into the world today?

This book is titled ***IMAGINEERING***. It helps you engineer your imagination to succeed in all walks of life. This book is a journey to create the whole '*You*' and to create better life experiences for *You, by You*.

I am on a constant journey to make myself whole, complete, and feel fulfilled. For the last 20 plus years of training, coaching, and transforming people and organizations, I realized the challenges we face result from the limitations created by our limited thinking. We may be aware or even unaware of these limitations; however, they strongly affect what we want and whether we succeed in getting it.

This book also shows how changing people's limitations, even the most straightforward limitation, can profoundly affect their personal and professional lives.

It is my privilege to share my findings from my life and the lives of many thousand people I have worked with. I have filled this book with stories, poems and sayings from my life experiences so you can better understand the concepts. (In all cases, I have changed the names and personal information to preserve anonymity.)

As you read through the book, it will work its own magic on you, and you will activate your own magic. Throughout the book, I have provided some exercises to help you make the conscious and unconscious changes that will lead to a decision. If you do these exercises, you'll be motivated to take action that will potentially affect your professional and personal growth. By letting go of feelings of uncertainty that prevent you from taking the necessary steps to achieve success on all levels of life, you will learn to empower yourself.

You will learn to identify and overcome your obstacles. You will discover the road to self-assurance, focus, and confidence to pursue your dreams and goals fully. To achieve the objectives you have set for yourself, you will acquire the skills necessary to operate at the highest levels of competence. You will regain your life's meaning and purpose. Your habits, core beliefs, daily routines, the people you surround yourself with, and the environment you live in is more important than genetics in determining who you are and what your life is today.

Every single one of us can be the best in the world at something. Let's together discover our best.

To get the best out of this book, I urge you to keep taking notes while reading and diligently practice the exercises given.

ACKNOWLEDGEMENTS

*S*ince I started my first job 23 years ago, I've learned and used nearly every tool, technique and strategy to control my emotions and change my mindset. My gratitude to my school and college teachers, my trainers, my coaching clients, my spiritual gurus, my bosses, my mentors and coach's who have contributed to my life's journey and through the many books I have read, and all my trainees and clients who have added to my journey of *Imagineering*.

I have delved deeply into the fields of neuroscience and neuropsychology over the past 15 years. I want to express my sincere gratitude to several amazing people who helped and encouraged me along this path.

Without my parents, Captain P K Vijayan and Mrs Veena Colleen Vijayan, who encouraged me and provided opportunities to develop into the best version of myself at all times, this journey would never have begun. My sister, Vinita Vijayan Chanan, for adoring me and supporting me in all my endeavours. My late grandmothers, whom I fondly call Ammuma and Nana, shaped my thinking as a child and a young adult and filled my life with beautiful memories.

My huge in-law family for understanding and supporting me. My life partner, Prabhakar Azad, is a constant source of love, support and care. You give me the strength to discover this journey and always support and encourage every endeavour of mine. And to our son, Ishaan, the depth of my love for you is impossible to express in words. The bond we share and the love and care I get from you are priceless. I'm so proud of you and deeply love you for who you are and who you are becoming. You are my inspiration to strive to become the best version of me.

I'm thankful to every one of those with whom I have had the joy to work with. My gratitude to all the organizations I have worked for, my supervisors, co-workers, trainees, coaching clients, and loved ones who have played a significant role in my journey. Even though I haven't mentioned you all here, you all know who you are and have contributed to this journey.

Last but not least, I want to express my sincere gratitude to God for always making everything possible and for making my life so beautiful.

CONTENTS

Section 1: The Fundamentals 1
  1. Clarity On Reality 2
  2. Without The Box Thinking! 15

Section 2: The Being 24
  3. Our Thoughts Become Things 25
  4. Are You Interested Or Committed? 38
  5. Mind over matter 47

Section 3: The Doing 62
  6. Powers We Have 63
  7. Transformation Journey 78

Transformational Coaching – FAQ's 98
Meet The Author 102

SECTION 1

THE FUNDAMENTALS

SUCCESS PRINCIPLE - 1

CLARITY ON REALITY

*O*ne of the most pervasive myths in our culture today is that we are entitled to a great life –that somehow, somewhere, someone (certainly not us) is responsible for filling our lives with continual happiness, exciting career options, nurturing family time, and blissful personal relationships simply because we exist.

But the real truth–and the one lesson this book is based on–is that only one person is responsible for the quality of your life.

That person is YOU.

If you want to be successful, you have to take responsibility for everything you experience. This includes the level of your achievements, the results you produce, the quality of your relationships, the state of your health and physical fitness, your income, your debts, your feelings–everything! This is not easy. In fact, most of us have been conditioned to blame something outside of ourselves for the parts of our lives we don't like. We blame our parents, bosses, friends, co-workers, spouse, the weather, economy, government, our astrological chart, lack of money–anyone or anything we can pin the blame on. We never want to look at where the real problem is–OURSELVES.

Let me explain this with a wonderful story.

Once upon a time, a young man named Jake always blamed others for his failures. He blamed his parents for not providing him with enough resources, his teachers for not giving him good grades and his friends for not supporting him enough.

One day, he met a wise old man who gave him a piece of advice that changed his life forever.

The wise old man said, ***"Transformation starts with YOU. Stop blaming others and start taking action."***

Jake took this advice seriously and decided to change his attitude. He started taking responsibility for his actions, and instead of blaming others, he started finding solutions to his problems. He worked hard, studied diligently and started making progress in his life. Soon, he landed a good job and started earning well. He even started a small business on the side and became successful in that too.

One day, Jake met the old man again and thanked him for changing his life. The wise old man smiled and said, "I did not change your life; you did it yourself. You decided to transform your life, and that's why you succeeded."

Moral of the story: ***Everybody can tell you to transform; however, transformation happens only when YOU decide to make it happen.***

You may feel you haven't produced the life or results you desire since you are the one who determines the standard of the life you lead and the outcomes you achieve.

None other than YOU has to make that decision.

To achieve major success in life and accomplish the most important things to you, remember:

TRANSFORMATION STARTS WITH "ME."

Over the years, I've worked on many business transformations. During this time, I've seen how critically important leadership is to transformation outcomes. And why is that?

Simply put, the leader is the catalyst for change.

He/she is the person who paints the vision of what "*different*" looks like and why "*different*" is better so that people understand the need to transform.

Without that vision, people will not transform.

I have seen that *transformation is human*.

In an organization, leadership is a key driver of successful transformation to point out specific behaviours that can lead to that success.

So, how can you become a highly effective leader of transformation?

The fact that you hold a leadership position does not necessarily imply that, by definition, you possess a vision, the ability to act as a catalyst, or the emotional intelligence necessary to bring other people along on the journey. On the other hand, some people in leadership positions naturally possess those qualities, but many others do not. Therefore, prior to beginning a project, evaluate and honestly reflect on your capacity to articulate the project's beginning to others and serve as a catalyst. It would be best if you do not prepare for failure before you begin. Self-analysis ultimately aims to cultivate skills if you discover you lack them.

Remember that even in a leader, transformation starts with "ME."

So, *personal transformation is a significant change or shift in an individual's thought and/or behaviour pattern.*

STEPS TO TRANSFORM YOURSELF

1. Know your current self and think of your future self

We can't begin any transformation without knowing our starting position. We also need to know who we need to become or what we need to accomplish. Any change starts and finishes along these lines. Yet, as a general rule, there is no closure since change isn't a status quo; it is a continuous process. Generally, a Journey into Transformation begins with dissatisfaction with one's current situation, a constant but quiet inner whispering that one could reach higher.

2. Know the purpose of transformation

That inner whisper allows one to seek deeper. When they do, one usually realizes they don't have a purpose for why they are doing what they are doing. But if you want to see a transformation in your life, you must have a purpose. If you stay on course, the purpose will become revelatory.

The journey that is transformation can be challenging; therefore, it is important to discover the "why" quickly and build a compelling purpose to transform.

3. Be encouraged by disappointments and be persistent

Any new change is wrapped with obstacles, and failures are an integral part of the transformation process. If you want to transform anything, you need to learn to accept failures and to learn from failures. The soul of transformation is focus and persistence. So, always remain focused and be persistent.

4. Transform voluntarily - do not force yourself

You need to love transformation and voluntarily transform your life. If you force yourself, you will be under stress, which isn't a good approach to change.

5. Support any actions that help you transform

You may wish to take many actions. However, take actions that only lead you to transform. Especially watch your behaviour and actions.

6. Be faithful to your choices and go all the way

We don't like to be betrayed by others. However, we often betray ourselves, which is why most transformations end after the first obstacle. Be loyal to your decision and believe in your abilities and yourself. Whatever you start, give yourself to finish. Don't look back; just look ahead and go all the way.

7. Keep tabs on your development and measure your improvement

Don't blindly get into any transformation. Know your current position, goal and where you are at any moment. When you track your progress, you are motivated to continue with that action. But if you have a period of regress, you need to change or readjust your behaviour or actions. Learn to measure your improvement, and when you create your metric system, you will know what to do more and what to do less.

8. Don't overthink - live your transformation

Experience the transformation process. It is more about how you carry on with your life. Deeds are more potent than any words. Transformation is a continuous cycle; however, that cycle needs positive change. In the existence of some individuals, better temperament, more energy, superior personal satisfaction, etc. are some positive changes.

OBSTACLES TO TRANSFORMATION

1. Asking, Why Me?

Lack of an Uplifting Outlook on this journey, continually victimizing yourself, feeling sorry for that "Why me?"

2. Lack of a Seeker's Mindset

This journey is about self-transformation. But if you hold yourself back and want spoon-feeding, it gets difficult. Many people like it easy; they want everything on their lap. They are unwilling to seek and understand reality for what it takes to get you there. This is an attribute worthy of development in a journey to transform.

3. Lack of Faith and Trust in a Higher Power

It helps if you have some faith in a power higher than us all, for we are all weak. We do need to hold onto something when the going is tumultuous and filled with uncertainty. Over the annals of his existence, man has discovered that, as an individual, he is frail and unaccomplished when faced with challenges. When he is filled with the deep knowledge that he is not alone, that same man can achieve what most, including himself, thought was an impossible act.

4. Lack of Self-Belief

There is so much need to deal with in this area. Many cannot trust their internal guidance since they cannot completely accept that they are exceptional for it. This can be a major block because their progress is next to impossible if they cannot trust and listen to themselves. Therefore, it is of the highest importance to develop a sense of self-belief, and it can begin with the smallest of things and gradually develop into bigger achievements. It would help if you believed that an integral part of the transformation is a journey from zero or low self-belief to extremely high self-belief.

5. Lack of Self-Love

This has more to it than it seems. From a very young age, we are programmed to believe that we are graded – regardless of who we are. Early on in school, we were good students if we did something well. If we behaved per the family norm, we were good children. Break that set of rules, and we were bracketed into segments. Finally, after much self-learning, one learns that "I" is not what someone else construes. It is about what one makes of oneself and what one builds accordingly. It is more about forgiving oneself for everything and embracing one's "self" with great love–someone who deserves the best, with a great amount of self-respect.

Value what you are blessed with. Accept what was not given. Live life to the fullest. Vibrate at the happiest and highest love frequency and explore and experience different things in life. Live to one's highest potential.

6. The Ego

Awareness of and working on it is critical. The subtle ego in this journey is a big drainer.

7. Lack of Understanding of Inner Work

Many people feel that inner work is meditation and healing, for which you must sit on the floor and close your eyes. One can say they did inner work when they introspected themselves constantly, identifying what was hindering their mindset and working on those inner issues consciously. That is inner work.

8. Attempting to control things - "Put conditions"

Numerous attempts to determine and rationalize things, for example, "the union should happen in 3 months" or "he should come to me then only…" block your energy big time because you don't know what you don't know.

9. Blaming others for your separation

Many feel their family, relatives, friends or karmic partners are responsible for their separation. Well, they might be playing their role so that it helps you in your spiritual journey, but they are not the ones who are a real hindrance.

If you can work on all the above factors, you have surrendered, putting yourself into the most favourable vibration to attract the union.

EXERCISE 1:

1a. What is your current reality? Where are you in life in the areas below? Rate yourself on a scale of 1 to 10, 10 being the highest and 1 being the lowest.

1b. Where would you like to be in the future in the areas below, say one year from now? Rate yourself accordingly on the parameters below:

1. Finance
2. Career and business
3. Health
4. Relationship
5. Contribution
6. Spiritual Growth
7. Recreation and Fun
8. Physical Environment

NOTES

NOTES

SUCCESS PRINCIPLE - 2

WITHOUT THE BOX THINKING!

*B*efore we get into the second principle, do the 9 DOT exercise given below to check your thinking pattern. Be honest with yourself.

Without lifting the pen connect 9 dots with 4 straight Lines. No overwriting any line

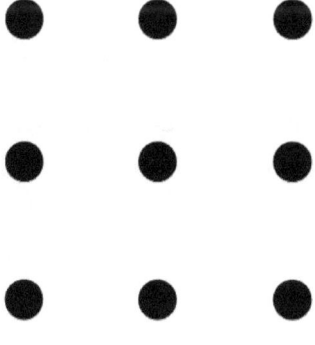

Once you have completed the exercise, reflect on what you did to connect the 9 dots. Did you get it easily in the first 20 seconds? What thinking pattern enabled you to complete the exercise?

So, what you just did was "think without the box." Do not limit your goals by looking at what you currently have. For example, you may think I live in a one-bedroom house kitchen. How can I possibly think of living in a bungalow?

As David Schwartz said, *"Believe Big. The size of your success determines the size of your belief. Think little goals and expect little achievements."*

So, how do we Think Big?

We have all been told by someone sometimes to "think out of the box!"

I say, practice **"*without-the-box thinking!*"**

So, what is "without-the-box thinking"?

I have illustrated it with a small diagram below.

The first box illustrates "thinking in the box," the second "out of the box thinking," and the third one "without-the-box thinking."

Without-The-Box Thinking

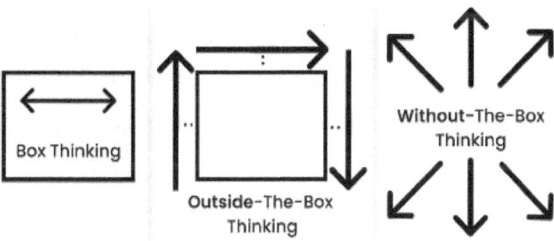

"Without-the-box thinking" is a concept similar to "out-of-the-box thinking" but takes it one step further by encouraging individuals to completely disregard the constraints or limitations that may typically be associated with a problem or situation.

"Without-the-box thinking" involves breaking free from established thought patterns and assumptions and considering completely novel approaches to a problem or challenge. It requires an open-minded and imaginative mindset, as well as the ability to challenge one's own biases and preconceptions.

Some examples of "without-the-box thinking" might include creating an entirely new business model, designing a product that completely disrupts an industry, or approaching a social or environmental issue completely unconventionally. Essentially, it involves pushing the boundaries of what is considered possible or feasible and embracing a willingness to take risks and explore uncharted territory.

Some examples of "without the box thinking" are:

1. Airbnb: Airbnb is a company that revolutionized the travel industry by offering travellers a unique and affordable alternative to traditional hotels. Instead of booking a room in a hotel, travellers can now rent out someone's spare room or an entire home for a more authentic and personal experience.
2. Tesla: Tesla is a company that has disrupted the automotive industry by developing electric cars that are stylish, high-performance and environmentally friendly. By thinking without the box and focusing on innovation, Tesla has become a leader in the industry.

Some ways that can help you "think without the box":

1. Challenge assumptions

Questioning assumptions is an important first step in thinking without the box. Don't accept conventional wisdom or traditional ways without questioning their validity.

2. Embrace creativity

Creativity involves thinking beyond what's been done before and exploring new possibilities. Look for inspiration from diverse sources and experiment with different problem-solving approaches.

3. Take risks

Thinking without the box often involves taking risks and stepping outside your comfort zone. Be willing to try new things and take chances, even if they seem unconventional.

4. Collaborate

Brainstorming with others can help you generate new ideas and perspectives. Seek out diverse viewpoints and be open to constructive criticism.

5. Keep an open mind

Finally, keep an open mind and stay flexible in your thinking. Be willing to pivot and adjust your approach as you learn and grow.

With these strategies, you can cultivate a mindset that encourages "without-the-box thinking" and leads to innovative solutions and breakthrough ideas to achieve your goals.

Now that you have understood the fundamentals of success, it's time to start creating your goals.

Exercise 2:

Below are 20 powerful questions to help create goals and transform your life.

Write your answers in the 'notes' section of this book.

20 Questions to Transform Your Life

Q1. If you could fully tap into your potential, what might be different from the current you?

Q2. How would your life change if every day you performed to your full potential?

Q3. What are the areas in your life where you feel you could be achieving more, and why?

Q4. What exactly would life look like one year from now once you have made the change in a particular area of your life?

Q6. What are some of the qualities in you that you would like to change in order to become an extraordinary person?

Q7. Why is this important to you?

Q8. How will your life change when you achieve this goal?

Q9. Who are people in your life whose life will change with you?

Q10. Who is the person suffering because of you?

Q11. What will you lose if you don't achieve your goal?

Q12. What will you gain if you achieve your goal?

Q13. What are the reasons you have not achieved your goal till now – challenges, obstacles, or hidden beliefs?

Q14. Which aspect do you want to focus on?

Q15. What are your goals for the next year?

Q16. What will happen once you have achieved your goal?

Q17. What will be the difference you see in yourself and around you?

Q18. How would you know you are progressing in the right direction? What are your milestones?

Q19. What would be different six months from now if each and every day you performed to your highest potential?

Q20. Why is achieving this goal important to you now?

NOTES

NOTES

SECTION 2

THE BEING

SUCCESS PRINCIPLE - 3

OUR THOUGHTS BECOME THINGS

I'm sure you have heard of the phrase "what we give more of, we get" means that the more we give of something, the more we are likely to receive in return. This concept can be applied to various aspects of life, including relationships, personal growth, and professional success.

For instance, in relationships, if we give our partner more love, kindness and support, we are likely to receive the same, or more, from them in return. Similarly, if we focus on personal growth and continually work on improving ourselves, we are likely to attract positive experiences and people into our lives.

In a professional context, if we put in more effort and work hard, we will likely achieve success and recognition. We will likely build stronger networks and attract new opportunities if we are generous with our time and expertise.

Overall, the phrase *"what we give more of, we get"* emphasizes the importance of being proactive, positive and generous in our actions and interactions with others. By giving more, we create a positive cycle of reciprocity that benefits us and those around us.

We are surrounded by and inside the life force. We are profoundly influenced by a vast ocean of energies we cannot perceive with our five senses. Life energy, also known as *"chi"* in Chinese and *"prana"* in Sanskrit, is one such energy. We move and interact in more than just the physical world of matter, which we are all familiar with. While our physical body may walk in the world of matter, a subtler part of us moves and interacts on a level of pure energy woven throughout our body.

We know from science that energy underlies everything. It is a fundamental component of all matter. The energy that makes up our bodies also makes up the bricks that make up our house. Energy makes up everything from our phones to our houses, animals and trees. It is all the same, changing shape and "flows" constantly. We are an essential component of the universe, so it is impossible for us to separate ourselves from it.

From a spiritual perspective, we are souls who never die and use a physical energy body to experience life on

Earth. The soul uses the body as a vessel, just like a driver controls a car. Since we and everything around us are made of energy, we must also be connected to everything. We are intertwined.

Going one step further will imply that our feelings and thoughts can make the world a better place. Thoughts of positivity can have an impact on those around us and travel through the energetic ether. Like a boomerang, we will receive more force for what we give.

The "boomerang," which we frequently regard as "coincidences," will return to us with positive events, people, and circumstances if we send out positive vibrations and reflect our true emotions and feelings. The same is true for negative thoughts and feelings like anxiety, resentment and so on. The "boomerang" will eventually catch up with us and bring us back to our negative experiences or events.

Let me illustrate this with a beautiful story.

A son and his father were walking in the mountains.

Suddenly, the son falls, hurts himself and screams, "AAAhhhhhhhhhhh!"

To his surprise, he hears the voice repeating, somewhere in the mountains, "AAAhhhhhhhhhhh!"

Curious, he yells, "Who are you?"

He receives the answer, "Who are you?"

And then he screams to the mountain, "I admire you!"

The voice answers, "I admire you!"

Angered at the response, he screams, "Coward!"

He receives the answer, "Coward!"

He looks at his father and asks, "What's going on?"

The father smiles and says, "My son, pay attention."

This time the father , screams, "You are a champion!"

The voice answers, "You are a champion!"

The boy is surprised but does not understand.

Then, the father explains, "People call this **ECHO**, but really this is **LIFE**. It gives you back everything you say or do."

Our life is simply a reflection of our actions. If you want more love in the world, create more love in your heart. If you want more competence in your team, improve your competence.

This relationship applies to everything, in all aspects of life. Life will give you back everything you have given to it.

So, what are you giving to life today?

Remember, every thought or action has an effect or consequence. The nature of that effect depends upon the nature of the cause. If the cause is good, the effect will be good. But, if the cause comes from negative thoughts or evil, the results will be equally negative or evil.

Therefore, as it is said, it is essential to:

"Watch your thoughts, for they become words;

Watch your words, for they become actions;

Watch your actions, for they become habits;

Watch your habits, for they become your character;

Watch your character, for it becomes your destiny."

This is your "Inner World"

OUR INNER WORLD DICTATES OUR OUTER WORLD WITH WHAT WE THINK.

According to quantum physics, everything vibrates; "everything" is energy, and our thoughts are powerful energy-filled cosmic waves. It appears that we are all one energy and a part of "a sea" of energy.

Because we are part of a universal consciousness, our thoughts are essential. We create the universe as we move through it by sending out cosmic waves through our thoughts and feelings.

Scientists tell us that the universe is rapidly expanding, yet no one can understand why. However, if we are part of the creation by using our thoughts and feelings in our inner world, it all makes sense. Religion and science are fast approaching each other. From a scientific viewpoint, experimental evidence suggests that we are all part of one mind, One Energy, and a Universal Consciousness. From a religious perspective, we are told that we are particles of God.

The more research our quantum physicists do in this field, the more they realize that there is a power greater than us—a universal power, a power of pure energy and pure consciousness.

The collective consciousness of humanity is the cause of the current state of the world. The average vibration from which humanity operates is reflected in the world's current state. Conflict, famine, fear, violence, hatred, frustration, and war exist within the human condition and can be found anywhere in the world. However, we are also witnessing change, love, kindness, expansion, forgiveness, and growth at the same time. This is taking place on the planet right now.

STEPS TO MAKE OUR "THOUGHTS BECOME THINGS"

1. Visualization

When we create a mental image of what we want, we are more likely to attract it into our lives. By visualizing a desired outcome, we focus our thoughts and energy on that outcome, which can help us manifest it.

2. Belief

Our beliefs shape our reality. If we believe something is possible, we are more likely to take action to make it happen. Conversely, if we believe that something is impossible or that we don't deserve it, we may unconsciously sabotage it ourselves and prevent it from manifesting.

3. Emotions

Emotions are powerful tools for manifesting. We vibrate at a higher frequency and attract more positive experiences into our lives when we feel positive emotions like joy, gratitude and love. Conversely, when we experience negative feelings like fear, rage or sadness, our vibration decreases, and we attract negative experiences.

4. Action

Thoughts alone are not enough to manifest our desires. We also need to take action towards our goals. When we take consistent, inspired action, we send a message to the universe that we are serious about our intentions. We are then more likely to see results.

Overall, thoughts become things through a combination of focused visualization, positive beliefs, high-frequency emotions and inspired action. We can manifest our dreams by aligning our thoughts and actions with our desires.

So, now that you have understood that we are energy bodies, *what energy are you carrying today, tomorrow or anytime at all?*

The following is a quote by Thich Nhat Hanh, the father of Mindfulness.

"Every feeling is a field of energy.

A pleasant feeling is an energy which can nourish.

Irritation is a feeling which can destroy.

Under the light of awareness,

the energy of irritation can be transformed into the energy which nourishes."

So, how do we ensure that, at all times, we stay positive and give out a pleasant feeling?

It is important to recognize that it is not realistic or healthy to always try to stay positive. Everyone experiences a range of emotions, including negative ones, which is a normal part of the human experience. However, by cultivating a positive mind-set, we can stay positive most of the time.

SOME TIPS FOR CULTIVATING A MORE POSITIVE MINDSET

1. Practice gratitude

Concentrate on the good things in your life and the things you value. This can help you focus on more positive thoughts instead of negative ones.

2. Reframe negative thoughts

Try to reframe negative thoughts in a more positive light whenever they occur. For instance, reframe the statement, "This is challenging, but I'm capable of finding a solution," as an alternative to "I'm never going to be able to do this."

3. Surround yourself with positivity

Spend time with people who uplift and support you and engage in activities that make you feel good. This can help create a more positive environment and mind-set.

4. Take care of yourself

Prioritize "self-care" activities like exercise, healthy eating and adequate sleep. You can improve your mood and outlook on life by caring for your physical and emotional needs.

5. Make Mindfulness a habit

Mindfulness exercises like deep breathing and meditation can help you become more aware of your thoughts and feelings and learn to control them better.

Remember that it's okay to experience negative emotions and that it's not realistic to try to stay positive all the time. However, incorporating these practices into your life can cultivate a positive mindset and improve your overall well-being.

Exercise 3:

1. Reflect on the thoughts that you think often. Are the thoughts negative or positive?
2. Every morning, write down a thought journal. Just open a blank page and write down all the thoughts that come to your mind at that present moment. Over a period of time, analyze what kind of thoughts you are thinking. Are they positive or negative? Are they about the past, present or future?
3. Once you have analyzed your thoughts, what actions are you willing to take to ensure you stay in the present and think positively?

NOTES

NOTES

SUCCESS PRINCIPLE - 4

ARE YOU INTERESTED OR COMMITTED?

Some years ago, when I was working at a hotel in Mumbai and was responsible for guest satisfaction, the human resource manager, Ms. Preeti Chawla, called me and said that a training program was happening in Pune the next week for which both of us had to go.

I was excited.

On the day of the program, we both took the Shatabdi Express train to Pune. We reached Pune station, and a hotel car was there to receive us and take us to the training venue.

It was a training program on "Improving Guest Satisfaction" at the hotel. I entered the vast conference hall, and the trainer, Ms. Shaw, started the training. I was fascinated by her training style, the way she spoke to the participants, the way she held everyone's attention, the engagement of the participants and the total involvement of each and every participant.

By the end of the program, I was mesmerized, and I told myself I wanted to be like her one day.

So, after the session, I walked up to her and thanked her for a fascinating session.

I told her, "I want to become like you one day."

She smiled at me and said, "Sure, you can." Then she asked me, **"Are you interested or committed?"**

I was puzzled, wondering what she had just asked me. What does it mean—interested or committed?

And then she said:

"If you are interested, you will only do the things that you like to do.

When things get tough, you will blame, justify and give excuses for why you can't do certain things.

But if you are committed, you will do the hard things, the things that you need to do. You will be willing to overcome all your excuses and justifications of blaming the government, the economy, the people in your life, your friends, your situation, and your environment."

That day, when I heard this, I thought that all the years of my life when I was working hard and struggling, I realized I was only interested and not committed. And because I was not committed, every decision of my life was not followed by the right action. Every time things got tough, I quit. Once I got this "aha" moment, it was only commitment all the way through.

Today, I am very successful thanks to Ms. Shaw for that question that changed my career and my life.

After that, whenever I feel like giving up on anything, I ask myself this question.

"Am I interested or committed?"

Earlier, every time I decided to change my life, I asked myself four ordinary questions:

Do I have money?

Do I have time?

Do I have support?

Do I have knowledge?

I noticed that every time I wanted to start something, I blamed it on not having time, money, support, or knowledge. Whether it was learning something new, writing a book, losing weight, or anything else, these were the four things that always came up.

These are the four sentences we all have fed ourselves from childhood, society, environment, culture and education system. Look around. There are people in the world who have no support, no time, no money and no knowledge, yet they have achieved their goals and created fame and a name for themselves. Everybody has 24 hours, and in those 24 hours, some people get the work of 72 hours done.

So, one day, I looked back on my life and realized I had kept telling myself these sentences all my life. I wanted to study further and grow in my life and career. I kept telling myself I didn't have time, had no support at home, and gave excuses. I have a family; how will I take care of my home? Where is the time to study?

And then, I kept asking myself the question, "Am I interested, or am I committed?" till it completely rewired my mind.

So, my questions to you today are:

Are you interested, or are you committed?

And if you are committed, how will you ensure you achieve what you want?

You can use my strategy to rewire your mind. Keep the word "committed" as your screen saver, or make it your password. Type it constantly, and make sure your fingers know you are committed. When you are committed, you will notice excuses will go away, and you will attract opportunities in your life.

We have much energy in our bodies. Our body is a machine producing electricity. We have trillions of hertz of energy inside us. It is only getting wasted on things we waste our time on.

So, there are three things you need to ask yourself to shift from being interested to being committed:

What do you need to eliminate from your life?

What do you need to continue doing in your life?

And what do you need to start doing in your life?

We live in an environment where we absorb over 40 thousand bits of data every single second. You can think of your brain as a data-processing machine. And this data processing machine, through your five senses– sight, touch, smell, taste and hearing–is absorbing more than 40000 bits of data every single second from our environment.

It need not necessarily come from areas we are focusing on. It also comes from areas that we are not focusing on. So, we need to eliminate specific data that is not useful to us. Now, if we are not conscious of the data going inside us, will we be able to eliminate it?

This data that we are processing is shaping up our lives. So, we have to be very <u>CONSCIOUS</u> of the data going inside. We have to be conscious of our <u>LIFE.</u>

We will go back to our environment once we put the book down. But we must be very conscious of our life for as LONG as we live, so we have to be a LEARNER.

Then only will we become a CLLL–**CONSCIOUS LIFE-LONG LEARNER.**

We don't want to be the floppy disk with the world moving so fast. I'm sure you know what I mean. We all want to lead a good life because we will live long lives. So, here's something interesting.

In the word "**LEARNING,**" another important word is hidden.

Can you figure it out?

There is "EARNING in "**LEARNING**."

Did you ever notice that? So, the more we are conscious about learning, the more we will earn a better life.

So, I want you to keep asking yourself all the time is: "***Are you interested or committed?***"

EXERCISE 4:

1. Reflect on all the tasks you started in your life and quit halfway through. What was the reason you did so? Were you interested or committed while doing those tasks?
2. What would you do differently now that you will be committed?

NOTES

NOTES

SUCCESS PRINCIPLE - 5

MIND OVER MATTER

*J*ohn Roebling, a creative engineer, had the idea in 1883 to build a spectacular bridge between Long Island and New York. However, experts in bridge construction all over the world considered this to be an impossibility. They advised Roebling to drop the idea as it was impossible to accomplish, unworkable and never before had it been done.

Roebling could not ignore the image of the bridge in his mind. He kept thinking about it and was absolutely certain that it was possible. He only needed to tell someone else about the dream. After much discussion and convincing, he persuaded his young son, Washington, an engineer, that they could build the bridge together.

The father and son came up with ideas for how they could do it and how to get around the challenges as they worked together for the first time. They hired their crew and started building their dream bridge with a great deal of enthusiasm, inspiration, and the thrill of a wild challenge in front of them.

A few months after the project started, John Roebling died in a tragic accident on the site. Washington sustained injuries that left him with some brain damage, rendering him unable to walk, talk, or even move.

"We advised them of this."

"Crazy men and the dreams they have."

"It is foolish to pursue irrational visions."

Everybody had a negative remark to make and felt that the venture ought to be rejected since the Roeblings were the ones in particular who knew how to construct the extension.

Washington's mind was still as sharp as ever, and despite his handicap, he never gave up on his goal of completing the bridge. He attempted to rouse and give his energy to some of his companions. Yet, they were too dismayed by the undertaking.

He could briefly see the sky and the tops of the trees outside as he lay on his bed in his hospital room with sunlight streaming through the windows. A gentle breeze blew the thin, white curtains apart. He appeared to be receiving a warning to persevere.

He had an idea all of a sudden. He decided to make the most of the fact that he could only move one finger. He gradually developed a language of communication with his wife by moving his finger. He contacted his wife's arm with that finger, demonstrating that he believed she should call the specialists again. After that, he instructed the engineers by tapping her arm similarly.

Even though it seemed foolish, the project was back on track. Washington wrote down his instructions with his finger on his wife's arm for 13 years until the bridge was built. As a tribute to the triumph of one man's indomitable spirit and his determination not to be defeated by circumstances, the magnificent Brooklyn Bridge stands today in all its splendour.

In addition, it is a tribute to the engineers' perseverance, teamwork and faith in a man regarded as insane by half of the world. It also serves as a tangible reminder of his wife's love and devotion, as she patiently deciphered her husband's messages and instructed the engineers throughout the 13 years.

Perhaps this is one of the finest examples of "MIND OVER MATTER"–perseverance in overcoming a severe physical handicap and accomplishing impossible objectives.

When we encounter challenges in our day-to-day lives, those challenges frequently appear insignificant in comparison to those faced by many others. We can learn from the Brooklyn Bridge that, despite the odds, one can realize a dream with determination and perseverance by giving it our 100 percent. If we give our 100 percent, we can realize even the most distant ambition.

When someone says they gave their 100 percent, they usually mean giving the task their full attention, focus and effort. It shows that one is completely dedicated to achieving the goal and doing everything in one's power to make it happen.

"Giving our 100 percent" means not holding back, not giving up quickly and persevering through challenges and setbacks. It also involves being proactive, taking the initiative and being accountable for actions and results. It also means putting in the necessary time, energy and effort to accomplish a task or goal and being fully present and engaged in the process.

At work, when I led a session on "Giving It Our All," many people asked me some really interesting questions. I'm sure you'd have questions of your own.

Q1. Which aspects of our lives require our full attention?

Giving our full attention to a particular area of our lives is largely determined by a person's priorities, objectives, and values. However, it is generally necessary to give 100 percent to the things that are most important to us, such as:

1. Relationships with others

We can foster trust, respect and love by giving 100 percent to our friends and family. This can help us form lasting, meaningful connections. In addition, it entails being completely present, actively listening, and demonstrating empathy and comprehension. Being supportive, respectful and communicating clearly and honestly are all part of it. Additionally, it entails a commitment to resolving disputes and working toward common objectives.

2. Work or career

Giving 100 per cent to our work or career can lead to professional growth, success and satisfaction. It can also help us develop new skills and learn from challenges. It will also help us advance quickly in our careers.

3. Well-being and health

It is possible to improve our physical and mental health by giving 100 percent to our health and well-being, such as regularly exercising, eating well and getting enough sleep. Doing this will make our lives more satisfying and enjoyable. It entails committing to maintaining your mental and physical well-being. It involves developing a strategy for achieving exercise, diet and stress management objectives. It additionally implies focusing on taking care of oneself and making a move to deal with our anxiety, getting sufficient rest and some margin for unwinding and happiness.

4. Personal growth

Giving 100 percent to our personal growth can help us develop new interests, learn new things and grow as individuals, leading to a more fulfilling and meaningful life. It also means setting goals, creating a plan, and taking action to improve our skills, knowledge and abilities. It involves being disciplined and committed to learning and growing and seeking out opportunities for self-improvement. It also means being open to feedback and willing to take risks and try new things.

Ultimately, it is up to each one of us to determine where we should give our 100 percent based on our unique circumstances and priorities.

Q2. Why is it crucial to give our 100 percent to whatever we do?

It is essential for several reasons:

1. Achieving our goals

When we give our 100 percent effort to a task, we are more likely to achieve the desired outcome. It helps us achieve our personal and professional goals and provides us with a sense of accomplishment.

2. Developing self-worth

When we put in our best effort, we feel good about ourselves, which can boost our confidence. It can assist us in approaching new challenges with confidence and optimism.

3. Improving relationships

Giving 100 percent to our relationships can help build trust, respect, and understanding, leading to more robust and meaningful connections with others.

4. Developing skills

Giving our best effort can help us develop new skills and learn from our mistakes. It can lead to personal and professional growth, making us more capable and confident in the future.

5. Being a positive influence

When we give our best effort, we set an example for others. We inspire others to do their best, creating a positive and productive environment.

Q3. How can we overcome obstacles that prevent us from giving our 100 percent to a task?

1. **Identify the obstacle:** The first step is to identify what prevents you from giving your best effort. Is it a lack of motivation, time constraints or a lack of skills or resources? Once you identify the obstacle, you can develop strategies to overcome it.
2. **Break the task down:** If a job seems overwhelming, try breaking it down into smaller, manageable steps. It can make it easier to focus on each step and give your best effort.
3. **Prioritize and manage your time:** If time constraints are an obstacle, prioritize your tasks and manage your time effectively. It may involve setting deadlines, creating a schedule or delegating tasks to others.
4. **Get support:** If you lack the necessary skills or resources to complete a task, seek consent from others who can help. It may involve asking for help from colleagues or seeking professional development opportunities.
5. **Stay motivated:** Sometimes, a lack of motivation can prevent you from giving your best effort. Find ways to stay motivated, such as setting goals, rewarding yourself for progress or reminding yourself of the benefits of completing the task.
6. **Focus on progress, not perfection:** Don't let a fear of failure or a desire for perfection prevent you from

giving your best effort. Focus on making progress, learning from mistakes, and continuously improving.

Q4. How do we prioritise tasks and allocate energy to ensure we give our 100 percent to the most critical tasks?

1. **Make a list of tasks:** List all the tasks you need to finish, including their deadlines and any other important information.
2. **Identify the most critical tasks:** Review the list and identify the most important or urgent tasks. These are the tasks that should receive your highest priority.
3. **Evaluate the tasks**: Evaluate the most important tasks based on their complexity, importance and urgency once you have identified them. It will assist you in determining the amount of time and effort you should devote to each task.
4. **Create a schedule:** Make a schedule that allows you to divide your time and effort efficiently. It could mean dividing larger tasks into smaller, more manageable chunks or setting aside specific times of the day for certain tasks.
5. **Focus on one task at a time:** Concentrate solely on one task at a time and avoid multitasking. It can assist you in giving your all and completing each task to the best of your ability.

6. **Take breaks:** Regular breaks can help you maintain energy and focus. Schedule breaks throughout the day and use them to recharge and refocus.
7. **Review and adjust:** Regularly review your schedule and task list to ensure that you are staying on track and making progress towards your goals. Adjust your schedule and priorities to give 100 percent to the most critical tasks.

Q5. What are some common mistakes people make that prevent them from giving their 100 percent to a task?

1. **Procrastination:** Putting off tasks until the last minute can prevent you from giving your best effort and result in rushed and unfinished work.
2. **Distractions:** Distractions such as social media, email and other interruptions can prevent you from focusing on the task at hand and giving your best effort.
3. **Multitasking:** You may not be able to give each task your full attention if you try to handle too many things simultaneously, resulting in a lack of focus.
4. **Lack of motivation:** A lack of motivation or enthusiasm for a task can make it challenging to give your best effort and complete the task to the best of your ability.

5. Overcommitting: Taking on too many tasks or responsibilities can overwhelm you and prevent you from giving full attention to any task.

6. Perfectionism: A desire for perfection can prevent you from completing tasks on time or moving on to new tasks, leading to a lack of productivity and a failure to give your best effort.

7. Lack of skill or resources: Having the necessary skills or resources to complete a task can prevent you from giving your best effort and lead to incomplete or subpar work.

Q6. How can we remain motivated to give our 100 percent in the long run?

1. Set goals: Setting clear and achievable goals can help you stay motivated in the long run. Ensure your goals are SMART: Specific, Measurable, Achievable, and Time-bound.

2. Divide tasks into manageable steps: You can keep yourself motivated and make progress toward your goals by breaking down tasks into smaller, more manageable steps.

3. Celebrate progress: Celebrate your progress along the way. Even small wins can help you stay motivated and engaged.

4. Find meaning in your work: Connect your work to your values, beliefs, or a larger purpose. It can help you stay motivated and committed to giving your best effort.

5. **Stay positive:** Even when you face difficulties or setbacks, it can be easier to stay motivated if you keep a positive attitude.
6. **Create a supportive environment:** You can stay motivated and focused by surrounding yourself with supportive people and creating an environment that supports your goals.
7. **Take care of yourself:** Taking care of your physical and emotional health, such as getting enough sleep, exercising and reducing stress, can help you maintain motivation in the long run.
8. **Learn continuously:** Continuously learning and improving your skills can keep you engaged and motivated in your work.

There are no guarantees in life, but you will always receive what you give. You will receive exactly what you give into something if you give it all your attention, energy and time. To ensure that you will receive everything you require, give everything you have. <u>Give your 100 percent to whatever you do.</u>

EXERCISE 5:

1. Think of a problem area in your life. It could be strengthening a relationship, a problem related to your work or career, health or any area of your life.
   a) What could be the reason for the problem?
   b) What actions would you take to come out of the problem?

NOTES

NOTES

SECTION 3

THE DOING

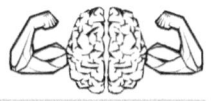

SUCCESS PRINCIPLE - 6

POWERS WE HAVE

I believe in the philosophy that

"WE CONTROL OUR FUTURE. OUR LIFE IS A PRODUCT OF THE CHOICES WE MAKE."

Let me explain this.

We all have three powers:

1. POWER TO DESIRE
2. POWER TO LEARN
3. POWER TO ACT and COLLABORATE

I'm sure you have seen an ant when it sees a crumb of bread or cake on a table. The ant has the power to desire the crumb. It also has the power to think; the crumb is big. "I cannot carry it alone, and I must call other friends." And, in no time, you see more ants on the table. They collaborate and carry the crumb away.

The ant has the power to desire the crumb, the power to think about it and the power to act and collaborate.

Now, do all these three powers that the ant has depend on any influential people in the ant's life? Does it depend on the ant's history or past or the trauma the ant went through in the giant world of humans? Does it depend on the rank of birth, gender or anything else? No, right?

SO, THESE POWERS ARE FREE.

And the ant is only a 2-dimensional insect. It can only move forward and backwards.

So, as humans, we also have these three powers and are 3-dimensional.

My question to you here, then, is:

Are we using these three powers diligently, or do we give these powers away by saying, *"I don't know how to do this. No one taught me. I didn't get the right education. I'm a woman. I'm a man. If I had more money, I would have built a bigger house. I can't do this, it's not my job, etcetera."*

So what are these? These are just excuses. We give away these powers by making excuses. When we give ourselves these excuses, we tell ourselves it cannot happen. Okay, let's forget whatever we have done in the past to give away these powers. Let's learn to re-embrace them.

There is one crucial thing we need to understand about our brain.

OUR BRAIN IS A PROCESSING UNIT

This processing unit is connected directly to our five senses, and through our five senses, we are constantly exercising the power to learn, whether we like it or not. Refer to the diagram.

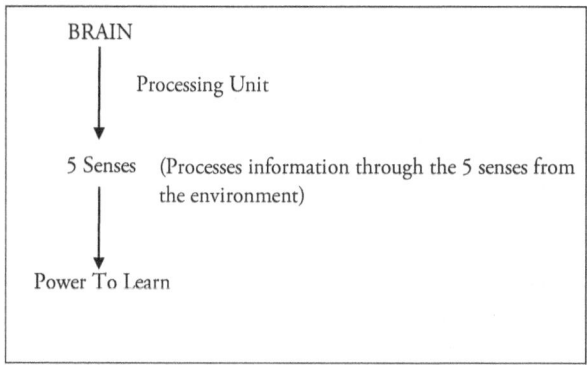

Our brain processes about 40 thousand bits of information every moment. The largest computer in the world processes some 1-5 billion bits of data every single moment. But our brain processes about 36 quadrillions of calculations every single moment. Isn't this something fabulous and miraculous?

So, there is a difference between us as humans and ants. In our evolution, we are much superior. We are on top of the life chain. So, there must be something better in us that has put us on top of the chain.

And that is our ability to **FOCUS.**

Sometimes, we all have the challenge of staying focused because of too many distractions around us. While some of us have learnt to bring our focus to the present moment, the question that arises is, what are we focusing on?

As we know, what you focus on expands! Unfortunately, you will realize that most of our focus depends on what is happening in our lives right now, and we don't know what our five senses are absorbing from our environment. All we know is that our five senses are plugged into the environment, and we are taking these inputs and processing the data.

Now, whatever is in your environment is getting inside you wherever you go or where your focus goes.

Now, reflect: are you noticing more problems in your environment than possibilities?

Our focus is majorly on the problems. There is nothing wrong with that because you want to solve them. That becomes counterintuitive for our brain for one single reason: we are learning machines, and so we are constantly learning.

That is why it is said, "We are a sum total of five people we spend time with and five books we read."

And this process is called **NEUROPLASTICITY.**

It is believed that our brain develops once we reach the age of 7. But that's not true anymore. Researchers have proved in the last 50 years that our brain constantly changes until we die.

Therefore, Neuroplasticity is the ability to form systems in the brain, which happens whenever we learn something.

This depends on two things:

1. Nature – what you are born with (body, skeleton, etc.), comprising 20 percent of your brain.
2. Nurture – what you pick from your environment comprises 80 percent of your brain.

The result of your life depends on 20 percent of your nature. But the neuroplasticity of your brain depends on 80 percent of the environment you are in. The environment controls 80 percent of your brain.

That's the power–your behaviour and thinking in your environment control patterns.

If your environment is old and not conducive enough to change, you will be sucked into the old environment.

But if you are a learning machine, do you understand the *POWER OF YOUR ENVIRONMENT?*

Therefore, if you want to change your life, you must change your FOCUS.

It is proved that when you reach a particular stage in your life, you can influence the environment and not let it influence you.

Let us understand this through a story.

A long time ago, in a joint family, there was a grandfather who was a very critical person. The son and daughter-in-law lived their life on their terms and didn't share anything with the grandfather. The grandson is watching all this. He is confused about the values of the family and wonders what is right. Now, the grandson likes both the grandfather and his father.

When the grandson grows up and goes into the world and is exposed to smoking, drugs and all other things, his father tells him that he is not supposed to do it. But the son thinks that when the grandfather said not to do certain things, the father went against the grandfather and did it in hiding. So that's the right thing to do, according to the grandson.

Now, this is how our environment influences us. So, if these five people are part of our environment, can we change this environment?

Yes, of course, by transforming ourselves.

Now if you are in my environment, I'm helping you transform, and when you transform, you can change your environment. As much as your environment impacts you negatively, it can affect you positively. Transformation does not happen in a few days. It is a continuous journey. When you transform yourself, you are transforming your environment too.

So, even if you impact one person, you have no clue how that person's life and the environment too will change. If you decide to impact the lives of your customers, team members and people around you daily, you have no clue how those lives will change.

Let me share an experience with you.

One of my coaches' was leaving her organization because her husband was getting transferred to another city. She was upset and didn't want to leave the organization as she had worked there for about 15 years. During one of our coaching sessions, we explored the possibilities for her to continue her career in the new city. She continued her sessions with me; today, she travels the world and trains people. Since I coached her, she knew she had to give her 100 percent to whatever she did.

On Guru Poornima, she called to thank me and said, "You made me a creator of my life."

Now, she went on and took action, and today, she is transforming the lives of hundreds of people with her training.

When you transform others' lives, they get inspired by your actions and, in turn, will transform many more lives.

We say leaders should walk the talk. *Are you truly walking the talk, or are you just walking and talking?*

So, how do we transform ourselves?

Let us briefly understand this by first understanding how our brain functions. Refer to the diagram below.

We have three layers of the brain:

1. The Reptilian Brain

The oldest layer of the brain is called the reptilian brain. It is about 7.5 million years old. It is composed of the brainstem, the structures that dominate the brains of snakes and lizards. Ninety-five per cent of all bodily activities happen on autopilot through this brain. It is related to thirst, hunger, sexuality, territoriality, habits, and procedural memory (like putting your keys in the same place every day without thinking about it or riding a bike). This brain focuses on surviving–safety, comfort, fight or flight. All our habits and behaviour happen through this brain. This brain is critical for us to move forward. Therefore, it is the 'Being Brain,' also known as the survivor.

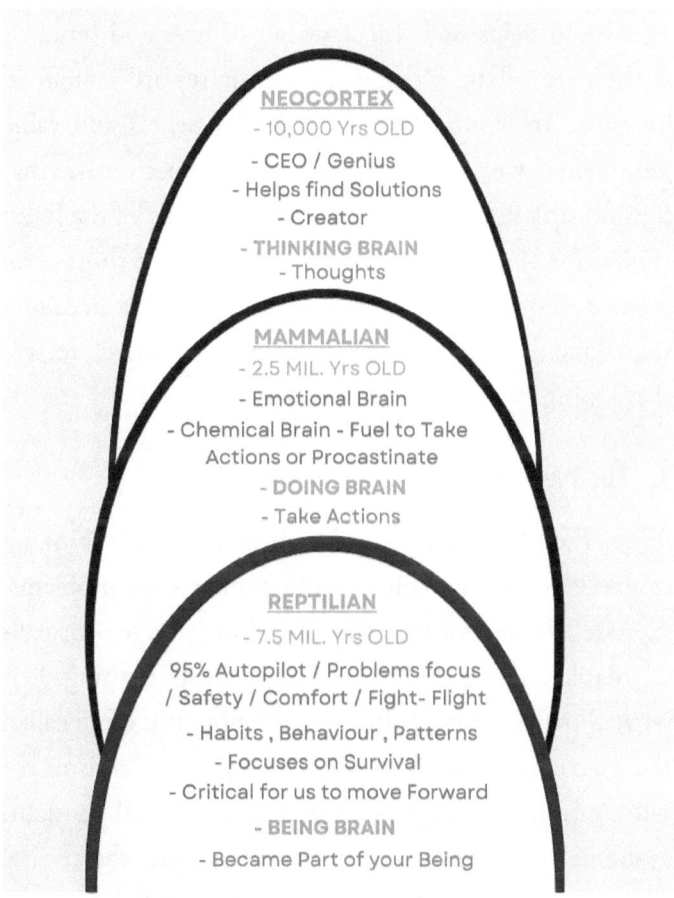

2. The Limbic Brain, also known as the Mammalian Brain

The limbic brain manages the body's limbic system. It developed around 250 million years ago with the evolution of the first mammals. It is responsible for "emotions" in humans because it can record memories of actions resulting in pleasant and unpleasant experiences. This brain helps us fall in and out of love and bond. It is the core of the pleasure system or reward system in humans. The limbic brain houses the beliefs and value judgments we form, frequently unconsciously, that significantly impact our behaviour. This part of the brain is vital for learning and memory, converting short-term memory to more permanent memory, and recalling spatial relationships in the world about us. Therefore, it is the 'Doing Brain.'

3. The Neocortex

It was the last 'brain' to evolve. It is the brain's thinking centre; it powers our ability to think, plan, solve problems, exercise self-control and make decisions. The neocortex is adaptable and capable of learning almost anything. It is what allowed human cultures to develop. It is often called the executive brain. It provides us with mechanisms for self-control, planning, consciousness, rational thought, awareness, and language. It also deals with the future, strategic and logical thinking and morality. It's the "minder" of our older, more primitive brains, and it lets us stop or inhibit reckless behaviour. This newer part of the brain is the part that is still under construction during adolescence.

Therefore, it is the thinking brain, also known as the 'Creator.'

Now that we have understood the three layers of the brain, let us understand how we can change any action into a behaviour.

Let's understand this with an example of driving a car.

In the beginning, you had thought that you must drive a car. That thought came into your Neocortex brain.

You obviously cannot read a manual and drive the car. You have to sit behind the wheel. When you did so, you did not master it in a day or two. You often looked down at the gear, brake, or accelerator and probably missed banging the car. Your emotions were either of fear, which then changed to confidence. And you continued to drive daily. All this happened in the 'Mammalian brain.'

Slowly, you got the confidence to drive alone; then you got the confidence to listen to music and drive, and eventually, you now have the confidence to drive without even wondering which gear to change. Now, the skill has become so effortless that it is in Autopilot mode. This now comes from the 'Reptilian Brain.'

So, you moved from thinking of driving a car to taking action and making it part of your 'Being.'

So, what did you do to master the skill? Simple, you took ***"Action."***

Now, reflect on how often you have started something and stopped it mid-way. And why did this happen? Only because you should have taken action to complete the task. So, converting any action into a behaviour begins by taking action. Then, much ***"Practice"*** is required to get into autopilot mode or become part of your 'Being.'

Remember, every time you tell yourself you can't do something, it is when you are not taking the necessary action and practice for it to become your 'Being.'

EXERCISE 6:

1. What habit do you wish to adopt or leave?
2. What action would you take to do so?

Prepare an action plan and stick to it by practising daily. Once you have achieved your goal, I would love to listen to your success story.

Connect with me at coach@vinishajayaswal.com

NOTES

NOTES

SUCCESS PRINCIPLE 7

TRANSFORMATION JOURNEY

*A*ll this while we have been talking about transformation/change. Although it is good to transform, is it easy? I don't think so.

No one likes change except a baby in a wet diaper. There may have been many times you started something and then left it in between or just struggled to reach the goal. There would have been times when you started your transformation journey and then thought, "Why did I take it up?" But once you completed it, you appreciated your efforts.

Have you ever wondered why we go through these thoughts in our transformation journeys?

What do we all go through once we embark on our journey to change anything in our lives?

Let's understand this through the story of the dragonfly.

Transformation Journey

A small colony of water bugs lived in a quiet pond below the surface. Far from the sun, they lived as a happy colony. Scurrying across the pond's soft mud for several months, they were very active. They saw that one of their settlements appeared to occasionally lose interest in going about with its companions. It slowly vanished, clinging to the stem of a pond lily until it could no longer be seen.

"Look! One of our colonies is climbing up the lily stalk," said one of the water bugs to another. "Where do you believe she's going?"

It slowly went up, up, up... The water bug vanished from view even as they watched. Its companions waited and waited, but it never came back.

"That's funny!" said one water bug to another.

"Wasn't she happy here?" asked a second.

"Where do you suppose she went?" wondered a third.

No one had an answer. They were all greatly puzzled.

At long last, one of the water bugs brought its companions together.

"I've got an idea. The person who ascends the lily stalk next must promise to return and explain where they went and why. We guarantee," they said.

Imagineering

One spring day not long after, the water bug who had proposed the arrangement wound up scaling the lily tail. Up, up, up he went. He had broken through the water's surface and fallen into the expansive, free lily pad above before he realized what was happening. He was surprised to look around when he awoke. He was in awe of what he saw. His ageing body had undergone a startling transformation. His movement revealed a long tail and four silver wings.

He felt the urge to flap his wings even as he struggled. The sun's heat soon removed the moisture from his new body. He continued to flap his wings, and all of a sudden, he was above the water. He had evolved into a dragonfly. He flew through the air in great curves, swooping and diving. In the new temperature, he felt like an exhibitor.

The new dragonfly eventually relaxed happily on a lily pad. He got a chance to look down at the pond. He was right above the water bugs, his old friends. Similar to what he had been doing previously, they were scurrying about. The dragonfly then recalled the promise. He flew down without thinking. He bounced off the water's surface when he suddenly hit it. He couldn't go into the water anymore because he was a dragonfly.

"I can't return!" He said in dismay.

"At least I attempted to go back. I just can't keep my word. None of the water bugs would recognize me in my new body, even if I could go back. I guess I'll just have to wait until they also turn into dragonflies. After that, they'll know what happened to me and where I went,"

And the dragonfly winged off cheerfully into its magnificent new universe of sun and air.

Now, this is the way the dragonfly transforms.

Each one of us also goes through a similar transformation when we decide to make any change in our lives. Let us understand what happens in our space when we embark on the transformation journey.

We now know that we must move from a 'Survivor zone' to a 'Creator zone' to transform any area of our lives. I'm sure you have made multiple attempts to do this and may have succeeded at times and failed at others.

Then, what happens? What goes on? Earlier, you learnt you were interested, but maybe you were not committed. Maybe you're telling yourself that something or the other comes up, and you can't do it.

Refer to the picture below as you read further.

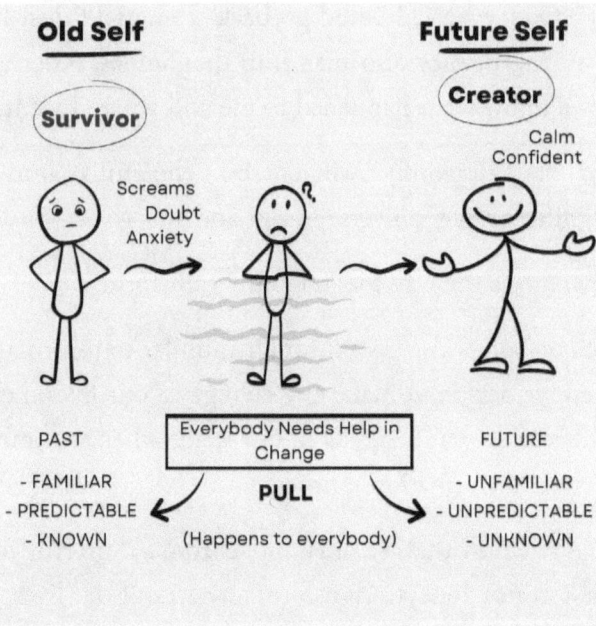

Between the life you're living as a survivor and the life you want to live as a creator, there's an ocean of change you must cross through to overcome all the conditioning you have gone through from childhood.

When you come into the middle of this ocean, you are in an unknown and uncertain territory. Think about it. You are in the middle of the ocean. You can't see the shore you came from, nor can you see the shore that you're heading towards. You are in the middle of the unknown, uncertain territory. And every time there is something unknown, your reptilian brain freaks out.

Unknown means fear and uncertainty. And when it is like that, the reptilian brain kicks in that this is unknown. This future is also unknown. Nobody has seen the future yet. It still needs to be created. Your mind starts tricking you. This shore is also unknown. I cannot see this.

This past is familiar, even if it's bad. And I know, so far in my life, I've handled all problems.

I have fought with them, or I ran away from them. So, this is something known.

The future is unfamiliar. Your mind starts tricking you, saying, "Go back, go back. This is unsafe; this is uncomfortable."

Even if there was a problem in the past, you still knew how to deal with it. And then, your reptilian brain started focusing on three things in your life:

1. On your body
2. On the environment
3. On time

When you focus on your body, you will come up with excuses: I don't feel like doing it today; my body is too tired; I'm feeling very sleepy today, etcetera. Reflect on how many times you have given yourself these excuses.

The second thing the reptilian brain will focus on when in the zone of survival is the environment–the people, the situations, how things are not right for you, how people are bad, and how nobody supports you, etcetera.

And the third thing you focus on is time because you know you are running out of time. Now, you want to know how long it would take to enter a safe environment. Then you tell yourself, "This time in the year, it's too late."

How often have you given yourself these excuses? And then, when the time comes to deliver, you get into emergency mode. And when you are in emergency mode, it's not the time to sit; it's not the time to meditate; it's not the time to eat or sleep. It's time to either run or fight. And you fight against what? Or you run away against what? The system. And that system is for you to create in this life.

As you read earlier, the four excuses you give are time, money, support and knowledge.

And when you freak out in that ocean of change, your mind starts playing tricks with you and telling you, "I don't have time. It's not the time to sit and think about new things. It's not the time to plan for my future. I don't have money. Where will I start the business? From where will I invest the money? From where will I learn new things? When I have money, I will do all those things. Investing in learning after education is a luxury."

Remember, you can never change your life if you cannot find the money for your learning. No amount of learning can change your life because that's an excuse you tell yourself, "Nobody supports me. Look, my family never supports me."

And then you tell yourself, "Only if I had the knowledge, I could have taken that opportunity, and I would have gone ahead and done what I wanted to do."

You are running all the time in emergency mode. And then when you are in that ocean of that emergency, you naturally start gravitating towards going back to your old habits, towards going back to your old behaviours, to your old choices.

Now, how do you break that cycle? Think about it. You are in the ocean of change. And now the excuses, all the blame, justification start coming: I don't have this, and I don't have that.

All of these are the RED FLAGS in your transformation journey.

Reflect on this statement: When you are alone in that ocean, you will freak out because you are not an expert swimmer.

But think about a situation where you have a transformation coach who is an expert swimmer. Now, you know you have a coach in that ocean of change.

When you start drowning, will you have more confidence because you're swimming under the guidance of a coach who will not let you drown? Now, you can cross the ocean of change with a coach around you.

Success is a team sport. You cannot be successful on your own if you're swimming in the ocean of change. It would help if you were supported by a coach who is already an expert swimmer. Remember, all successful people have a coach to guide them through the ocean of change.

That's where the entire philosophy of the Indian education system comes from–the Gurukool system, where the guru or the teacher, an expert swimmer, helps you cross that ocean of change. So, when you take support from the coach, transformation becomes effortless.

Now, you need to understand that when you get stuck in this change, you need to look at how your life is shaping up, what has happened in your life in the past, and how it will change.

You need to understand things about your life: some particular events that may have happened in your life have shaped the course of your life, and therefore, you have formed certain habits, behaviours or belief systems.

A lot of times, we bury those events. We do not allow ourselves to go through that experience or to remember those things so we don't get affected. How often have you buried certain things in your life that you do not allow yourself to be affected by?

Often, when I ask people, why are you not changing? Or why are you not successful? The reasons people give are that they lack opportunities or they lack luck.

Now, both are untrue.

We keep telling ourselves; I'm not lucky enough because I was born in an environment where I didn't have much money, I didn't have luxuries, I didn't have an abundance of anything, and the circumstances in my environment ensured I felt unlucky.

Now, reflect on where your focus is going. Is it going on your Negative Past or Positive Past?

To ensure it goes on your Positive Past, I want you to reflect on ten things you're grateful for in your life. It could be your body, your breath, the fact that you're waking up daily, your eyes opening, etcetera.

What are you grateful for in your life?

The next thing I want you to understand is the definition of Luck -

"Opportunities meet Preparedness."

If you are not prepared, the opportunity will not come to you. From here on, your job is to prepare for the opportunity, and then the opportunity will come to you.

Now onwards, every time you get that ocean of change and every time your mind plays tricks on you, remember to ask yourself the question we learnt earlier: *Are you interested or committed?*

This question will switch your gears, and you will start finding the support, you will start finding that money, and you will start finding that time.

You always have the time; you always have the money; you always have that support; you always have that knowledge. But you don't value it, or it's not your priority. And that's the reason why you're interested and not committed.

You keep giving yourself those excuses. And, remember, a lot of times, people are waiting.

People are waiting for somebody to change their life. People are waiting for something to happen to change their life.

Remember, *"If you are waiting, you are NOT creating."*

Your environment is more powerful than your willpower. So, always check on your environment. Because you know your dreams will become your reality when you change your inner world - your thoughts, feelings and behaviours.

You can stop halfway, and a lot of people do that. That's also a decision–stopping halfway, not going to the finish line.

How many times have you stopped halfway in your life?

But then you have to keep asking yourself this question are you interested, or are you committed?

Confidence comes from taking action, not decisions. Your decision is only a decision when it precedes action.

If there is no action, there is no decision. And when I say this, you might develop resistance in your space. So here is a process to overcome resistance.

When you are in the ocean of change, much of that resistance to running away will come up. So, it will keep bringing up anxiety, fears, and doubts. Why me? Why not me? This is not for me. I don't relate to this. This doesn't resonate. This is for somebody else.

All of that will come up. And we want to deal with that resistance in the most constructive, healthiest way. I will teach you a process you can use for the rest of your life to deal with any resistance in your space.

First, we must understand that whenever you get any fearful thought, it's at the thought level first. From the thought, it comes to feelings, and from the feelings, it comes to choices and then experiences, and so and so forth.

SQUASH TECHNIQUE

Before I explain the squash technique, let's understand how our brain learns.

When our brain learns, it is learning from our five senses.

1. Visuals - the way our eyes pick up information
2. Auditory - What we hear
3. Touch - we can call it kinaesthetic also
4. Olfactory - the smells of things we get
5. Taste

Now, when we are transforming our brain or retraining our brain, the first three senses are majorly involved in transforming our brain. And we are going to use these three senses in the squash technique.

After you read the complete process, please do it. Please don't do this process if you have any wrist or hand issues.

You need to stand up for this process, ensure you have nothing around you at one arm's distance, and keep your eyes closed throughout the process.

Step 1 – Close your eyes. Reflect on what resistance comes to you when you're in the ocean of change. Is it anxiety? Is it fear? Is it self-doubt? Is it confusion? Laziness procrastination?

Step 2 – Scan your head to find out in which part of your head is the thought or belief. You may feel a heaviness or a headache in some part of your head or even the whole head.

Step 3 – Imagine that you are **pulling out that thought** or belief from that part of your head and placing it on the palm of your non-dominant hand in front of you. Do the action that you are imagining.

Psssttt…. Don't pull your hair; pull the thought out.

Step 4 – Bring your dominant hand from behind you while you see that thought in the palm of your non-dominant hand in front of you and **SQUASH it** now.

Squash it as if you're killing it, literally.

You're killing it, and you're minimizing it.

If you do this right, your hands and palms will have a tingling sensation.

Your entire body will shift. Do it ten times before you stop.

What you did here is that you used the three senses. Visual, auditory and kinaesthetic. You visualize killing that thought. You heard the sound of that clap that you're killing that thought. And the body felt that sensation.

If you do this right, your entire body will feel warm, like you are sweating. Your breath has changed. Your heartbeat has changed. And look at your body posture. Do you feel more power in your gut right now? Notice how you feel.

When your brain is rewiring, your body is rewiring. Remember, your subconscious mind is in every cell of your body. You want to remove it from every cell of your body. If you want to increase this intensity, add a sound you don't like. Like an ambulance sound? Or a screeching sound? Or hitting the nail or dental work or something similar.

While you're killing that thought, you can play that sound in your mind. It will become even more irritating. Practice this at least ten times a day. Please make a list of all your limiting beliefs or thoughts and squash each one of them.

You can also SQUASH any bad habit that you wish to leave. It works well. So, now make yourself a commitment that you will do it ten times a day. What we are doing here is changing our body's biochemistry. And the moment the chemicals in our body change, everything changes. It's mind over matter because we can change our lives just by the thought.

We can change our bodies, environment and lives just by the thought. And it is not just possible for only the mystics or the sadhus and gurus, but it's possible for everyone. And I want to make it possible for every single human being on this planet.

I don't want to make it mystical because when we think of thoughts changing life, we think of those mystics' hidden knowledge. That's not true. We can all get there.

So, my job as a transformation coach, an NLP master practitioner, a facilitator, a trainer and an author is not just to tell you what is possible but to show you what is possible in real time. My suggestion is don't believe a word I say. Practice and see the magic unfold.

You can also **Book a One-Hour Free coaching session with me NOW**. I would love to hear about your experience after going through this book.

Connect with me at coach@vinishajayaswal.com

■ EXERCISE 7:

1. List 25 things you are grateful for in your life.
2. Daily, when you wake up, write down ten things you are grateful for. Before you go to bed, write down three things you are grateful for in the day.
3. Reflect on a transformation journey that you embarked on but never completed. What are the reasons that stopped you from completing it? Squash each one of those reasons.
4. Start a new transformation journey. It could be one that you started on earlier and left halfway through. Create small milestones to achieve weekly, fortnightly or monthly.

   Squash any limiting belief that will come your way.

"It's not how much you know. It's about how much you Own by Doing."

– Vinisha Jayaswal
Transformation Coach
coach@vinishajayaswal.com

NOTES

NOTES

TRANSFORMATIONAL COACHING – FAQ'S

*M*any of my clients need help understanding what Transformational Coaching is. So, I have answered a few 'Frequently Asked Questions' that my clients usually ask me on the first call. Feel free to get in touch with me in case you have more questions.

What is Transformational Coaching?

Transformational Coaching facilitates personal growth and development by helping individuals identify and achieve their goals, overcome limiting beliefs and behaviours, and live more fulfilling and purposeful lives.

Unlike traditional coaching, which primarily focuses on improving performance in specific areas, transformational coaching aims to bring about fundamental changes in an individual's mindset, values, and behaviours. It is a holistic approach that considers all aspects of an individual's life and encourages them to take responsibility for their own personal growth and development.

Transformational coaching uses various techniques and tools to help individuals gain greater self-awareness, challenge their limiting beliefs, and develop new ways of thinking and behaving that support their goals and aspirations. It emphasizes the importance of personal values, purpose, and vision. It encourages individuals to align their actions and decisions with these elements.

Ultimately, transformational coaching aims to help individuals achieve lasting and meaningful change, leading to greater happiness, fulfilment, and success in their lives.

What are the benefits of hiring a Transformational Coach?

Hiring a transformational coach can benefit individuals seeking personal growth and development. Here are some of the key benefits of working with a transformational coach:

1. **Gain greater self-awareness:** A transformational coach can help you better understand yourself, your values, and your beliefs. Through this increased self-awareness, you can identify any limiting beliefs or behaviours that may hold you back and develop new ways of thinking and behaving that support your goals and aspirations.
2. **Set and achieve goals:** A transformational coach can help you set and achieve specific goals that align with

your values and purpose. They can help you break down your goals into smaller, manageable steps and provide accountability and support as you achieve them.

3. **Develop new skills and behaviours:** A transformational coach can help you develop new skills and behaviours that support your personal growth and development. This may include communication skills, time management, self-care, or any other areas you wish to improve.

4. **Overcome challenges and obstacles:** A transformational coach can help you identify and overcome any challenges or obstacles preventing you from achieving your goals. They can guide and support you as you navigate difficult situations and help you develop strategies to overcome them.

5. **Increase confidence and self-esteem:** Through personal growth and development, working with a transformational coach can help you increase your confidence and self-esteem. You can learn to trust yourself, your abilities, and your decisions, leading to tremendous success and fulfilment in all areas of your life.

Hiring a transformational coach can be a valuable investment in your personal growth and development, helping you achieve lasting and meaningful change in your life.

What are you waiting for, then?

Hire your coach NOW…

Contact me at coach@vinishjayaswal.com

PRAISE FOR THE AUTHOR

"*IMAGINEERING* by Vinisha is a must-read for anybody who wants to transform their lives and achieve success.

Each topic and the examples in the book are presented in a clear manner and with utmost simplicity. It gets one to be reflective and gets one to act on it.

The book was an eye-opener for me.

If you wish to make a positive change in your life, try the book. It would be a transformational experience.

A bundle of tools to engineer your imagination.

The author is creatively elaborating on the 7 Success Principles.

I enjoyed the use of reflective questions, quotes and poetry that has been interwoven with timeless wisdom to tap into both the left and right brain faculties to enable transformation."

Deep Ahuja Sharma
ICF MCC
Partner – TPC Leadership
Founder – www.coachncoachee.com
Author – Deep Insights, Mentor Coach, ICF
Transformational Leadership Coach Trainer.

"*Imagineering* closely explores the transformation journey (inner and outer) that one needs to undertake in order to emerge successful.

Imagineering elucidates strategies for individuals to empower themselves and take appropriate actions through exercises and questions.

Each chapter will enrich your wisdom culminating in an empowering call to action for all those who want to be committed to success, not just interested.

Vinisha's attempt to help bring a renewed purpose and meaning to people's lives is well reflected in the book."

Dr. Sriharsha A Achar,
Chief Human Resource Officer,
Star Health and Allied Insurance Co. Ltd.

"I am awestruck by the depth of understanding of the contents that lead to each of us reaching our potential to be the best of ourselves.

With stories and personal worksheets, Vinisha has rightly emphasized that "transformation starts with ME" through "without the box thinking." There is a universal truism that "our thoughts become things" when we are "committed and not just interested." Being the best of ourselves is a case of "Mind over matter. Our belief in the "Powers we have" helps us chart our very own "Transformational Journey."

Vinisha has successfully deciphered the code of Life's 3 C's - Chances, Choices and Change.

I would highly recommend everyone to make a choice to take a chance on *IMAGINEERING* and bring about positive changes in your lives.

Her mentees are blessed to have her as their life coach.

Matharani Mathias,
Advisor – NITTE
Institute of Hospitality Services
Former Principal and Director of
Sarosh Institute of Hotel Administration

This book, *IMAGINEERING*, is on a very relevant topic which will inspire and ignite readers. All the topics and examples quoted in such a lucid form with so much simplicity are remarkable. This book would act as a lighthouse to direct towards the inner engineering, and when applied, our lives would be transformed.

I found the book eminently interesting, relevant and stimulating. I am sure and confident that every reader will emerge with something to think about and a lot to apply.

A word on Vinisha, whom I have known for over a decade. Vinisha is an accomplished L&D professional and a transformation coach. Her exposure has given an inside-out perspective on the book. What sets Vinisha apart are her passion to learn and her quest to understand the human mind dynamics and processes to get to the underlying core.

Break your chakravyuh by practising the seven success principles and give wings to your imagination; think big and fly high!

Shyam Iyer,
Founder and CEO
60 Bits Consulting
Ex – CHRO TATA Power SED

www.ingramcontent.com/pod-product-compliance
Lightning Source LLC
LaVergne TN
LVHW041852070526
838199LV00045BB/1569